DEDICATED TO

Helen Moore Noonan

1896–1976

* * *

and for

Ruth E. Rockwell & Thomas K. Noonan

Very special thanks are given to William Porter and the faculty of the Department of Journalism, University of Michigan, for their interest in and encouragement of a non-traditional graduate student; to Jean Campbell, Dorothy McGuigan and the staff of the UM Center for the Continuing Education of Women, to the UM Department of English and particularly Hilda Bonham and John Aldridge of the Hopwood Room. The deepest appreciation is tendered Gene B. Wilson and the staff of the Ann Arbor Public Library and the University Graduate Library for their valuable help since 1945. In addition, thanks are due Stephen Dunning of the University; himself a poet, he directed the Poetry Reading project at the university, 1976-1977.

GOOD COMPANY— POETS at Michigan

edited & with photographs by
Jeanne Rockwell

introduction by Sheridan Baker

NOON ROCK

THOMAS EDWIN NOONAN, PUBLISHER

1500 Longshore Drive

Ann Arbor, Michigan 48105

First Edition
LIBRARY OF CONGRESS CARD CATALOG NUMBER: 77-91403
ISBN 0-9602934-0-X

Library of Congress Card Catalog Number: 77-91403

ACKNOWLEDGEMENTS

The following poets and publishers are thanked for their very kind permission to reprint: For *Thinking of Seclusion*, from *Old Man Rubbing His Eyes*, by Robert Bly, copyright by the author, 1975, Unicorn Press, Greensboro, N.C.

How It Is, © copyright by Maxine Kumin, 1975, first appeared in the March 3, 1975 issue of the *New Yorker*, reprinted by permission © 1975, *The New Yorker Magazine,* Inc.

Happy In Sunlight by William Stafford, copyright by the author, from *Braided Apart*, by Kim and William Stafford, Confluence Press, 1976, Lewiston, Idaho.

Love, Another Story, by Gayl Jones, copyright by the author, 1975, appeared first in *Blacks On Paper*, a literary magazine published at Brown University and reprinted in the Brown Alumni Monthly.

Clouds by Philip Levine, copyright by the author, from *Red Dust*, Kayak Books, 1971.

A Year In Toledo by Carolyn Balducci, copyright by the author, 1977.

Mother's Past, by Reed Whittemore, copyright by the author, 1976, first appeared in the Sept–Oct 1977 issue of American Poetry Review.

From Room to Room, by Jane Kenyon, copyright by the author, 1977, is the title poem from her book of that name, Alice James Books, Boston, Mass. It first appeared in *The American Poetry Review*.

O Cheese by Donald Hall, copyright by the author, first appeared in *Grove*, winter 1976.

Ursa Minor by Beth Copeland, copyright by the author, 1977.

The Leaf-Eater is reprinted from *A Particular Place*, copyright 1969 by Dabney Stuart, with the permission of Dabney Stuart.

Making Music by Judith Minty, copyright by the author, from *Lake Songs and Other Fears*, by permission of the University of Pittsburgh Press, © 1974, by Judith Minty.

Vademecum by Lemuel Johnson, copyright by the author, 1977, from *Hand on the Navel*, Ardis Press, Ann Arbor, Michigan.

Sonnet XIII by Gillian Bradshaw, copyright by the author, won the Bain-Swigget award in the summer 1975 University of Michigan Avery Hopwood and Jule Hopwood contest.

Poem For People Who Came From the Moon by Duane Niatum © copyright by the author, 1973, reprinted from *Ascending Red Cedar Moon*, with permission from Duane Niatum and from Harper & Row, Publishers, Inc. New York.

Why I Never Answered Your Letter © copyright 1974 by the author Nancy Willard, from *Carpenter of the Sun* reprinted with permission of Nancy Willard and Liveright/Norton, Publishers, Inc. New York.

Lines to My Father © copyright by the author Sam Hamod, 1969, reprinted with permission from *The Holding Action*, 1969, Seamark Press, Iowa City, Iowa.

#3245 Introvert Poem by Margaret Kaminski, copyright by the author, first published by the Fallen Angel Press, Detroit, 1976.

Wringing Necks by Bert Hornbeck, copyright by the author, 1976.

Phoenix by Carolyn Holmes Gregory, copyright by the author, 1977.

Mathematician VIII/LXXVI, by E. G. Burrows, copyright by the author, 1976.

Dance Song by Anne E. Waldman, © copyright by the author, was first published in *Journals & Dreams: Poems* by Anne Waldman, Stonehill Publishing, New York, 1976.

The Great Bass by Richard E. McMullen, copyright by the author 1975, was first published in *Chicken Beacon*, Poems by Richard E. McMullen, Street Fiction Press, Inc. Ann Arbor, Mich. 1975.

Michigan Winter by Bobbee L. Valleau, copyright by the author, 1977.

Father O'Meara's Indulgence by Warren Jay Hecht, copyright by the author, first appeared in Vol. I, 1973 *The Periodical Lunch*, published by Street Fiction Press, Inc. Ann Arbor, Mich.

Cutting Back, by Joyce Peseroff, © copyright by the author 1977, is reprinted from *The Hardness Scale*, by Joyce Peseroff, by permission of the Alice James Poetry Cooperative, Inc., Copyright © 1977 by Joyce Peseroff.

Trial By Full Moon, by Andrew G. Carrigan, © copyright by the author, 1975, is from *Babyburgers*, published by Street Fiction Press, Inc., Ann Arbor, Mich., 1975.

Love, the Barber, is from *The Osprey Suicides* by Laurence Lieberman © copyright by Laurence Lieberman, 1973, reprinted with permission of Macmillan Publishing Co., Inc. from *The Osprey Suicides* by Laurence Lieberman © copyright 1973.

GOOD COMPANY

CONTENTS

"One merit of poetry few persons will deny;
it says more and in fewer words than prose."

Voltaire

FOREWORD

Poets are people from every walk of life, not unlike their readers. This particular book began in my mind when members of a class I was teaching made some sharp comments about the dull form of their poetry text. They were enthusiastic about poetry but wanted to know more about the people who had created the poems, just who they were, how the poems came into being, what the poets looked like, even what they did for a living when they weren't writing poetry.

In addition and significantly, these young people wanted to write poetry themselves, to read it aloud and discuss it.

This is a heartening reaction for those of us who enjoy reading and writing poetry. Even if what we write is done as occasional verse, translating as it does deeper, hidden feelings about an event or an individual, the sum of such effort is a valid form of communication.

The poets in this book represent the widest range of intellectual thought and background. They are not tied to any one particular section or school, though all have in some way been influenced by the Great Lakes region, either by being born here or by travel here to teach or to read their work before their peers and the public. Some are just beginning careers; others are at mid-point and some are internationally known writers. In every sense their work is quite literally good company

J.R.

INTRODUCTION

Poetry is popular, or so it seems to have become in the last two decades. The handful of students once invited to the professor's parlor to sit at the feet of an occasional gray poet has grown to thirty, sixty, eighty, and more—with the public sometimes swelling audiences to over a thousand. No doubt Ann Arbor and the University of Michigan's poetry readings reflect trends across the nation, but they also reflect a kind of affectionate tradition and special vigor. Jeanne Rockwell, a writer and photographer, attracted like many another to the University's readings, has represented them well in this collection.

Michigan's feeling for the importance of poetry must have gained some impulse when Longfellow published his *Hiawatha*, his "Indian Edda," portraying Michigan's Ojibwas, on the Lake Superior shore between the Pictured Rocks and the Grand Sable River. It may even have gathered some kind of slanting lustre from Julia Moore, "the Sweet Singer of Michigan," as she styled herself, the farmwife who wrote of how little Libby choked to death on a piece of beef (she "found no relief") and how the Reverend Mr. P. P. Bliss went "beneath the wheel of tide" in "The Ashtabula Bridge Disaster." Mark Twain parodied her, adding some fame, in *Huckleberry Finn.* And Detroit's own Edgar Guest had thousands of daily readers and loyal followers for a lifetime—"It takes a heap a livin."

But the poets in this volume represent not popular poetry but the popularity of poetry, and a local tradition of valuing it. Robert Frost was the University of Michigan's first poet in residence (1923–24), followed the next year by Robert Bridges, then Poet Laureate of England. Frost returned many times for talks and readings and visits of varying length, forming attachments still alive in the community. His portrait as a young man here hangs in the University library. W. H. Auden came for a year in 1939, leaving a less extended legacy from his single year, but one that includes a namesake, Wystan Stevens, son of faculty friends and now Ann Arbor's historiographer. Donald Hall and Radcliffe Squires have long taught and written on the University faculty, and have given many readings—Hall especially, who drew together a small group of townspeople known as "Poetry Ann Arbor" to sponsor readings by himself and others in elementary and high-school classrooms around the state to spread the enjoyment of poetry. Joseph Brodsky has defected from the U.S.S.R. to the University, where is now a Professor of Slavic, reading his poems in Russian and English to large audiences across the country. Robert Hayden, from Detroit with an M.A. from the University of Michigan, has been poet and teacher on the faculty from 1969 until 1976 when his appointment as Consultant in Poetry to the Library of Congress took him to Washington as the first black so appointed in a line of twenty-three distinguished predecessors.

The University's Hopwood Fund has stimulated the interest in writing of all kinds at the University of Michigan since 1930. James Avery Hopwood (Class of '05), who went from undergraduate extravaganzas to musical comedies on Broadway, left a fortune to his mother and the University to endow annual prizes in the drama, the essay, fiction, and poetry—evidently to promote the serious writing he never achieved. Eminent men and women of letters throughout the country serve as judges and give the annual lectures, as the committee annually divides more than $30,000 among the winners.

In addition, beginning in 1968 under the direction of Bert Hornback, public readings sponsored by the Department of English and the University's Extension Service have filled the halls in the Undergraduate Library or the Michigan Union with students and townspeople, among them Jeanne Rockwell, ready with her appreciation and her camera to render tribute to all those she missed by the following representation from those she didn't.

Sheridan Baker
The University of Michigan

THINKING OF "SECLUSION"
after Tu Fu

I get up late and ask what has to be done today.
Nothing has to be done, so the farm looks doubly good.
The blowing maple leaves fit so well with the moving grass.
The shadow of my writing shack looks small beside the growing
    trees.

Never be with your children, let them get stringy like radishes . . .
Let your wife worry about the lack of money!
Your whole life is like some drunkard's dream!
You haven't combed your hair for a whole month!

                                    ROBERT BLY

HOW IT IS

Shall I say how it is in your clothes?
A month after your death I wear your blue jacket.
The dog at the center of my life recognizes
you've come to visit, he's ecstatic.
In the left pocket, a hole.
In the right, a parking ticket
delivered up last August on Bay State Road.
In my heart, a scatter like milkweed,
a flinging from the pods of the soul.
My skin presses your old outline.
It is hot and dry inside.

I think of the last day of your life,
old friend, how I would rewind it, paste
it together in a different collage,
back from the death car idling in the garage,
back up the stairs, your praying hands unlaced,
reassembling the bites of bread and tuna fish
into a ceremony of sandwich,
running the home movie backward to a space
we could be easy in, a kitchen place
with vodka and ice, our words like living meat.

Dear friend, you have excited crowds
with your example. They swell
like wine bags, straining at your seams.
I will be years gathering up our words,
fishing out letters, snapshots, stains,
leaning my ribs against this durable cloth
to put on the dumb blue blazer of your death.

MAXINE KUMIN

Maybe it's out by Glass Butte some
time in late fall, and sage owns the whole
world. Even the obsidian chips
left by the Indians glitter, out of
their years. Last night's eager stars
are somewhere, back of the sky.

Nothing where you are says, "It's me
only." No matter how still the day,
a fence wire hums for whatever there is,
even if no one is there. And sometimes
for luck, by neglecting to succeed that day,
you're there, no one else, and the fence wire sings.

WILLIAM STAFFORD

LOVE, ANOTHER STORY

I turn the desk light off,
and the light of the room,
and close the door,
as if I belonged there.
"Thank you for packing the rest of my things," he says.
At the station. He has on blue dungarees.
"I dreamed I'd met you for the first time.
I said, 'Hi.'
You said, 'Speak.'
I said, 'Hi' again.
You said, 'Speak again. State your business. Why you're here?' "
"What did you say?" he asks.
"I said, 'I came because you said come.' "
"Did I answer that?" he asks.
"No, you just stood watching me."
He turns a bit away from me,
keeps his hands in his pockets.
Then he says, "We won't write.
Not unless there's something you feel you
have to tell me."
"There'd be no use in waiting, then, would there?" I ask.
He says, "No."
Then he says, "I don't think I'm a very good person."
"Neither do I," I say.
He frowns.
I'd meant, "Neither do I think I'm a good person."
But he took it wrong.
I let him keep it wrong.
He says quietly, "There's a story by Cervantes
about a man who went crazy
and believed he was made of glass
and wouldn't let anyone come near him
because he believed he was made of glass
from head to foot."
"Is it true?" I ask.
He doesn't answer, then he says,
"People aren't as fragile as they pretend to be."
When he shakes my hand,
I see his splintered glass for fingers,
the blood on my own.

GAYL JONES

7

CLOUDS

I
Dawn. First light tearing
at the rough tongues of the zinnias,
at the leaves of the just born.
Today it will rain. On the road
black cars are abandoned, but the clouds
ride above, their wisdom intact.
They are predictions. They never matter.
The jet fighters lift above the flat roofs,
black arrowheads trailing their future.

II
When the night comes small fires go out.
Blood runs to the heart and finds it locked.
Morning is exhaustion, tranquilizers, gasoline,
the screaming of frozen bearings,
the failures of will, the tv talking to itself.
The clouds go on eating oil, cigars,
housewives, sighing letters,
the breath of lies. In their great silent pockets
they carry off all our dead.

III
The clouds collect until there's no sky.
A boat slips its moorings and drifts
toward the open sea, turning and turning.
The moon bends to the canal and bathes
her torn lips, and the earth goes on
giving off her angers and sighs
and who knows or cares except these
breathing the first rains,
the last rivers running over iron.

IV
You cut an apple in two pieces
and ate them both. In the rain
the door knocked and you dreamed it.
On bad roads the poor walked under cardboard boxes.
The houses are angry because they're watched.
A soldier wants to talk with God
but his mouth fills with lost tags.
The clouds have seen it all, in the dark
they pass over the graves of the forgotten
and they don't cry or whisper.
They should be punished every morning,
they should be bitten and boiled like spoons.

PHILIP LEVINE

A YEAR IN TOLEDO (Four Poems)

1.

Cold black lake sky/line
Glass City postcard
Snap! What a shot!

2.

Gray grass, black earth
Lilacs frozen by the April snow,
Look at the birdie, Death,
Death, give us a smile!

3.

When the sun scorches lamplight
Run inside, Girl, leave the orange street
For the chill white walls,
The tint of song, the water lily,
Bukarahs rolling miles deep.
Let's talk till dawn.
A pink kiss ("Amor")
A golden, dusty saint or two, let's
Lie upon the marble floor and laugh.

4.

And we—
    we, ladies of the Garden Club—
We plant
    each fall we plant ourselves
We stake a claim on spring
    (though winter is humidified.)
Still, we plant—
    we dig, we get the stuff inside our shoes,
    between our toes, etched in our palms.
The worms can be trowelled away today,
And so, we plant.

CAROLYN BALDUCCI

Mother's past is full of old cars with very large fenders
Against which the young are leaning in knickers and caps
And very large skirts and fixed smiles
As the photographer, who is mother, puts the end of her finger
On the edge of the lens says Please Don't Move
And then moves, pushing the button.
In a moment they will be gone out the driveway waving,
Chugging into the future with dust rising
And kerchiefs floating out wildly over the fenders,
All gone except mother who now clambers
Up the rickety steps to the porch where she sits in a rocker
With her Kodak.
But the snapshots have none of that, only the fenders
And fixed smiles, only the moments
Very far back when everyone stood
As still as they could and tried not to blink
So that those who came later could look and say, yes it was
Like that then, just like that, including Ma's finger.

So it was like that. A book full of fenders.
  But was there not more?
  Ask yourself as you flip through the pages, the Martians,
  Where are they? And the funny crepuscular organs of dream
  sheep?
  It was on the first of July in aught-seven,
  As Ronald was walking home from the office at even,
  That he saw at the end of the street, partly hidden by bushes,
  What appeared at first to be Jesus but was not Jesus,
  But Charles Darwin.
  And then there was Aunt Mathilda who departed her mind
  In the sweets shop and no one had film. And so many
  So many others boiling and stewing
  In time's pot, they were missed by the Kodak
  Too. How many were missed?
  Ask.
  Ask how many were missed that it takes to make a good
  Past for a life or a book.
  The answer is always more pictures than poor mother took.

REED WHITTEMORE

12

Here in this house, among photographs
of your ancestors, their hymnbooks and old
shoes . . .
            I move from room to room,
a little dazed, like the fly. I watch it
bump against each window.

I am clumsy here, thrusting
slabs of maple into the stove.
Out of my body for a while,
weightless in space . . .
                        Sometimes
the wind against the clapboard
sounds like a car driving up to the house.

My people are not here, my mother
and father, my brother. I talk
to the cats about weather.

"Blessed be the tie that binds . . ."
we sing in the church down the road.
And how does it go from there? The tie . . .

the tether, the hose carrying
oxygen to the astronaut,
turning, turning outside the hatch,
taking a look around.

JANE KENYON

In the pantry the dear dense cheeses, Cheddars and harsh
Lancashires; Gorgonzola with its magnanimous manner;
the clipped speech of Roquefort; and a head of Stilton
that speaks in a sensuous riddling tongue like Druids.

O cheeses of gravity, cheeses of wistfulness, cheeses
that weep continually because they know they will die,
cheeses as blunt as gray rock,
cheeses of victory, cheeses wise in defeat.

Esrom as fundamental as a village family;
Pont l'Eveque intellectual, and quite well-informed; Ementhaler
decent and loyal, a little deaf in the right ear;
and Brie the revealing experience, instantaneous and profound.

O cheeses that dance in the moonlight, cheeses
that mingle with sausages, cheeses of Stonehenge,
cheeses of the Pacific Ocean, cheeses of new grass,
cheeses with gold threads like the threads in tapestries.

Reblochon openly sexual; Bresse Bleu like music in October;
Caerphilly like pine trees, small at the timberline;
Port du Salute in Love; and Caprice des Dieux
eloquent, tactful, like a thousand-year-old hostess.

O cheeses that are shy, that linger in the doorway,
eyes looking down, cheeses spectacular as fireworks,
cheeses of Lascaux, of bison carved in stone, cheeses
fat as a cushion, lolling in bed until noon.

Camembert distant and formal, then suddenly laughing;
Gruyére an old neighbor returned for a visit; Leiderkrantz
fresh and ebullient, jumping like a small dog, noisy;
and Dolcelatte, always generous to a fault.

O village of cheeses, I make you this poem of cheeses,
O family of cheeses, living together in pantries,
O cheeses that keep to your own nature, like a lucky couple,
this solitude, this energy, these bodies slowly dying.

DONALD HALL

Okuma San,
Your gold tooth mirrors sunlight
From the dark cavity
Of your mouth.
Plump hands trap
Escaping laughter.
I run to you, my knee daubed
With mud, with blood, your muffled laughter
Swathed in the thick gauze
Of your hands, run to you, my fists
Curse in a language
Neither of us understand.

Okuma San, little she-bear,
Alone among persimmons and pots and pans,
Crying to my mother about the crazy man
Who watches you hang out our clothes, who watches
The windows where blue-eyed strangers jab
Metal prongs into their mouths and speak
In a tongue as brittle
As glass.

Entering your narrow lodgings,
I inhale pungent *sashimi, sushi,*
The sweet steem of rice
Boiling into starch
On the hotplate.
I take off my shoes and tiptoe
Upon *tatami* as worn as sand, listen
To the spirals of your breath weaving steam
As you read to me from painted books.
I rest in your fat lap, drowsy, your voice a vessel
That carries me into the pictures, to places deep,
Buried inside a ripened peach, where words
Are seeds, and language
Is the page turning
In your hand.

BETH COPELAND

18

THE LEAF-EATER

The wind-sacked beast
Chugs and whines across the campus lawn
Sucking up the leaves in ordered rows
Before the first freeze and the winter snows.
A man says to himself, stifling a yawn,
They seem to have fallen for this raucous feast.

He watches from his office. Since quitting-time
Last night dogwood and elm did as they always do,
Dropping what was lifeless, coming clean,
While that machine
Cooled off in the shed, deflated and askew,
Hungover from its swinish pantomime.

But, again this morning, swollen like a sow,
It gorges on dead leaves, and its own noise,
So loud his thoughts go haywire. The childish
Fantasies he had cast off as trash
Heap up, tempting his windy hunger. A voice
Says *Eat,* and he fills the vacuum made by his old vow

To think austerely, dropping his green schemes.
Though dry at first, this fare
Suddenly turns sumptuous as spring
Beneath whose trees, ardent and flourishing,
The ghost of a boy turns cartwheels, unaware
He lives beyond the seasons of his dreams.

DABNEY STUART

20

Tuesday afternoons in the cave of our basement
my mother, like an organist,
sat in front of the old white mangle,
her music heaped in a wicker basket beside her.
I saw the flash of fur under her arm

as she lifted a sheet, folded it twice, and with her knee
moved the pedal that made her instrument go.
I watched wrinkles feed into the mangle, heard a hiss
as heat met dampness of muslin, smelled soap under scorch,
saw clean hymns flow out of the roller.

I have no talent for music, am not my mother.
Two hours by car from Kalamazoo to Muskegon
I sit behind the wheel, direct my instrument
along a white line, around curves, over rises;
my pedal maintains a tempo of seventy miles an hour.

Headlights rest on the fur of dead animals, and my wheels
roll over them: rabbits, cats, squirrels
pressed into the sheet of highway. It is a long drive home.
The hum of my motor blends with the thump of bodies
and the static rock beat out of the radio.

JUDITH MINTY

From *Hand-on-the-Navel*

I	IV
Red Bones	*In Paradisum*

vademecum
for a lapsed catholic
for Carty Caribbean
eating ashes in
a tight mouth,
for lent and passion
and meat runs
from bone gone red
shellscraped from
bone meat gone red
though you talk
and chant for
space in the mouth,
Carty Caribbean,
for baseless joy
in fire and water
baptism that turns
the white bone red
O the gleam of their
alabaster soul
cracks in cold water
what you eat
what you eat
the joy of it goes
away; and what
O red bones
will you do?

did you;
O would you
sail up in
a cannibal river
where the long
gorillas mate
once a year?
O Carty Caribbean
what ark holds back
such a deluge
red bones gnawed
by the life to come.

* * * *

LEMUEL JOHNSON

SONNET XIII

Fireflies embroider dreams upon the night
Between the dark and dark the flicker glows
In tones of pale beryl, of amber or of rose:
A swiftly-piercing needlepoint of light
That dwells an instant only within sight
Between the midnight blackness and twilight's close—
In the midst of motion rests the second of repose,
As the fire holds an instant in the flight.
We behold an instant and we know in part
A vision between the waking and a sleep
A glance of Heaven waiting on the heart
At light to surrender or in shadows keep.
A moment only—and how soon the vision fades
And lies forgotten under day-time's shifting shades.

GILLIAN BRADSHAW

POEM FOR THE PEOPLE WHO
CAME FROM THE MOON

Deer meadows end where wind
Settles in the city's heart of mushrooms;
River willow echo Snoqualmie chants
To children chasing quail into the afternoon.
Within their longhouses rising from the sea,
Carriers of the dream wheel
Sing their rain songs to the stranger.

When the evening logs burn down to masks,
Hunters from the sky enter
The spruce canyons of the dream, sleep
In the light that mutes both fern and village.

Having circled the lake for the dawn,
Blue mallards land on the bow of a lost canoe.
Elders with family buried under
Thundering clouds from here to the waterfall,
Put their ears against the rotting cedar,
Hear hoofbeats of deer and elk
Pound tributes in their veins:
The pulse of a moon with many seasons.

*Snoqualmie: A Salishan tribe living in Western Washington. Their name means "people who came from the moon."

DUANE NIATUM

It's true I make books, but not often.
Mostly I am always feeding someone,
nine cats whose tails flag me down each morning
and who know a soft touch when they feel one,
and who write on my door in invisible milk:
Good for a handout. Good for a night's lodging.

Mostly I'm taking Peter and not paying Paul.
My man comes home, dreaming of sirloin.
I ravage the house: three eggs and half a potato.
I embalm then in amorous spices with beautiful names.
It's true I make books, but mostly I make do.
The chapters of hunger are filled but nothing is finished.

At night a baby calls me for comfort and milk.
Someday I'll teach him to sing, to dance, and to draw,
to learn his letters, to speak like an honest man.
Right now I teach him to eat, and I tell him a story,
how an angel came to Saint John with a book in its hands,
saying, *Take and eat. It shall make they belly bitter,*
but thou shalt know all people, all prophets, and all lands.

NANCY WILLARD

LINES TO MY FATHER
(assassinated, Gary, Indiana, Oct. 1967)

My Father is watching over his Mosque, silently
He hovers now, praying;
My father is sitting on the step watching,
Holding his chest where the bullet entered his prayer,
Holding on, the maple trees blurring in his eyes,
He cannot rise, he is praying as his blood comes,
My Father is planting maple trees beside his Mosque,digging each
    hole
Carefully, patiently knowing the trees will grow,
He is watering the grass outside his Mosque at 3 a.m.,
His work is done and now my Father is covering the grass with
    love.

My Father is moving East, to Leb'nan, eating Kib'be, his
Mother offering him grapes and shade,
He is walking in the mountains, drinking water;
My Father is setting on a park bench beside me
Taking the air, watching my children in the grass,
He is talking of water,
He is trying to rest
But he must go, his Mosque is waiting.
My Father, dreaming of water when wakened,
when I found him, had only blood in his mouth.

SAM HAMOD

#3245 INTROVERT POEM

I sit in the dirty water of the bathtub watching the little red splotches on the insides of my knees, wondering what they are. The pearl nail polish wears off my toes. My cosmetics, if any, are usually ten years behind because I do not buy new ones and I do not throw the old ones away. I remember a picture of myself in a topless go-go outfit, my hair teased and ratted out in all directions, sprayed, exaggerated; thick black eyeliner all around my eyes. The pearl nail polish wears off and my heels harden from walking home from Jefferson Avenue.

I sit in the dirty water of the bathtub and think of the man I saw. I suppose I should call him a brother, but there is no name for anyone now since they all wear their hair long. I remember the pictures of the brothers in the paper in 1970. They had picked up hitchhikers and cut off their heads.

I sit in the dirty water of the bathtub and think of the man with the harmonica and guitar. He thought it was ten years ago and that he was Bob Dylan. He said, "Hi," but I thought he was crazy. I remember thinking, though, that I am equally crazy, hawking feminist hawking magazines like a hawk. Sold 100 this week. This is the best time to sell: everyone lies in the grass and smiles. Everyone smiles because I do not ask those who would not smile. Some of the men are angry because I do not ask angry-looking men if they want to by a feminist magazine. So then I ask, "*Do you want to buy a feminist magazine?*" "*No!*" they answer angrily.

I sit in the dirty water of the bathtub feeling my heels soften.

MARGARET KAMINSKI

WRINGING NECKS

Life being what it is
and a chicken's neck
these modern days
wrung by machine
and the body held
by an economical defeathering
frustrator
there must be kids who've never seen

so I should describe
what death was
for a chicken.
After you lost your head

wrenched by a hand
with a rotary motion
and the body flung off in an arc
you landed on your feet

and walked about
sensible enough
in wobbly circles
until the agony of life
and protest against the pot
were over, or enough.

It was self-respect
that made being a chicken count.
It was the power of walking about
even when they had your head.

BERT G. HORNBACK

PHOENIX

Give me a sip from
your loving cup
oh guardian angel
head up there, santo bello
give me synergic rhythm
to madness, method
coiling the genes.

This is the new age of reason.
So do not break sticks
to reckon fate's friction
nor pass me over
for fiction in the giant
diary of god.

Angel of parsecs
teach me how to hold
pen as sword
dissecting surgical the chaos
calling directions
to rid this world of tremor.

For goodness sake
I promise work
pax nobilis
you recollect the rushes
as life begins
to dig into a metaphor
this wedding takes on wings.

CAROLYN HOLMES GREGORY

Equations to him were cowboy sixguns
and holy writ. He wrote schoolwork
in a book like girls' names.
When I showed him my catch
he discovered the sign for infinity
on the underside of a leafwing.
At the owl's hole he spoke in awe
of the origins of zero.

In the long days when you were young,
strange friends moved next door
and moved away, trailing their hands
from car windows. You swore
never to forget them,
whoever they were.

As for him, he wears
a gown trimmed with moons and stars
and lives in a cave
with a skull, a bat, and a candle
or was it he
who this month lowered
a great spider through the roof of Mars?

E. G. BURROWS

DANCE SONG

To Expel Hesitation   *after the Copper Eskimo*

I am quite unable
to sing & stomp as he does, I am quite unable
& to play the string as she does sweetly
I am quite unable I am quite unable
I am quite unable
to move the sovereign forest, I am quite unable
& to turn the waves against the moon
I am quite unable I am quite unable
I am quite unable to dream the faun

I can measure
I can fasten
I can climb
I can slow my terrestrial clock

But I am quite unable to end this suffering
& bring you home
I am quite unable
I am quite unable

I am quite unable to impress as they do
I am quite unable I am quite unable
& to dress myself in furs & jewels
I am quite unable
I am quite unable

But I can heal
I can revive
& I won't wince with pain

I am quite unable to wince more pain
I am quite unable I am quite unable

ANN WALDMAN

43

THE GREAT BASS

Tonight the fisherman tells of the great
bass, pulled out of Houghton Lake
thirty years ago. The flesh
of the bass, eaten the same night,
has moved through many systems; now
its cells lie lost in other
things far from any water.
Yet in the fisherman's dark aquarium
brain, the great bass swims
and grows in the midst of thousands. Most
are only keepers; most are only
part of a catch; some are beauties
like the bass. They share that instant
when the water flowed away,
when the straight, hurting line led them
struggling to the light. Tonight
it is the bass's time again:
he lies in the weed bed; he sees the fly
touch the water; he moves to the bait.
Longer, heavier, stronger now,
he puts up the best fight yet.

RICHARD E. MCMULLEN

The desolate landscape returns
Pallid white;
A study in the colors of a corpse,
Imprisoning every field in view, the flatlands
Unrelieved by the haunted trees.

Old food lies rotting in the corners; papers and dust
Scattered across the floor.

Useless, and the fire dies out and we cannot chop the wood.
Unmovable, and we are frozen like the trees.
Death, we are.
Christmas never came.
Our bellies grow larger, but we do not feed them.
Christmas never came.

BOBBEE L. VALLEAU

FATHER O'MEARA'S INDULGENCE

Though disinherited I am a younger grandson of a man who dissolved his own eyes, died rotten to the nostrils with coercian and cocaine, a hypocrite whose self-disfeaturement subtracted with each small breath a shallow stench from his cancerous essence, etched his life into a true monument to the faceless dead. Despite his rationalization I am not an emulator of the lower class, but number in my company the late King Frederick IX of Denmark, royal appreciator of our real mortality. The consent to surgery Grandfather could not bribe from me whittled his jaws from his teeth while my granite resistance to medical vandalism allows my love to flower as Grandfather putrifies the very walls of his unfortunate coffin.

I am made rich, not in the monies withheld by his dishonest will, but in the timeless symbol of beauty germinated when the tattooer's needle breathed onto my skin the indelible vine that strangled my birthright.

My moralistic colleagues often wonder aloud what impelled a man of my reserved calling to suffer a stainless brush in lieu of the painter's sable and incorporate an object d'art into my torso instead of my living room. To them I say "To thine own self be true", and do not hesitate in reminding them that the velvet rose I prize so highly cost only the twenty-two dollars Anthony charged to embellish my breast, not the two hundred and fifty odd thousand the insensitive old man forbid me in the name of discretion.

What propriety would replace the sweet pain Michelangelo gladly embraced in the Sistine's inspired vault with the saccharine chemistry of convention? Men are rightfully tortured only by the fading of our individual existences, as Leonardo would be wracked by the failure of the experimental pigment that robs us of his divine vision of Our Lord's last but everlasting supper, not by stagnant custom.

Our bodies are our synagogues. We sing hosanna not in our throats, but from the depths of our bowels. The sacred adoration of life is not conducted under dead canopies of glass and stone, but must bloom in the fragile church The Savior chose for that ultimate worship. By adorning ourselves with The Creator's gifts—His birds, beasts and blossoms—we do not seek, as Grandfather falsely believed, to improve upon His finest work struck in the image of Himself, but dearly acknowledge the limitless, actual wealth He bestowed that we should live at peace.

WARREN JAY HECHT

CUTTING BACK

My coleus wag their purple tongues
like mean children. I take up
the pruning shears & the black rubber glove
& cut where the woody stem goes soft & green.
I shape what has gone wrong, like a surgeon
or interior decorator. Some cuttings I save
for the garage sale; the rest lie with chicken bones
& soup cans, looking like a mistake,
the child locked in the family freezer.

You say you're going on a diet
though I can pass my hand through your ribs
& play the Lost Chord. You'll survive
on green translucencies of lettuce,
slices of cucumber, sampling the song
of a warrior who eats
the heart of his hero & calls it devotion.

I break a lunch date. Examining myself,
I find a lump under my left breast,
a secret bud next to my heart.
I don't tell anyone.
At night, I plead fatigue; mornings I am up
before dawn. In a week, it goes away.

JOYCE PESEROFF

the error is thinking someone should pay
a point of blood rose round one end of the scalpel he held
parallel to the ground between his index fingers
his foot on the coffee table   the night sprinkler
swishing through the grass   the wide expression
in his eyes indicates an answer   but the syllables
keep coming apart in his mouth   he was   he thought
as he had been from the first   an idiot
to piece the sounds together in some fashionable
intelligence is the weight of the accused   the jury
must not doze

    "the trail house is on the mountain's
back"   he began   from this they were to conclude
that the shadow would keep the snow intact   hence
the purse could not have fallen into enemy hands
of its own volition

    "again"   he continued   "i tried
slinging my lungs into the valley   again   i am ashamed
to say carnations repulsed the attack how was i to
explain myself?   i had prayed i had collected marbles
i had put my deodorant in a vault   still the evidence
seemed overwhelming i must say it   the rainbow that
rises from water passes through two worlds as in death
we descend through all the lives we keep in our heads
layer by layer until we become what our children
inherit"

ANDREW G. CARRIGAN

LOVE, the Barber

I.

Love, the barber, shaves the night fields.
He trims the forests. Between his blades

Fall waves of the sea. They calm themselves.
Whatever falls away grows back in another

Place, in sleep. Beautiful hanks. My wife
Cuts my daughter's hair. Oh, it hurts my eyes

At first. Sweet face, you look so bare.
The brute has severed locks of sleep, and weightless

Dreams are falling fast, oh fast; the floor
Is strewn with waves of softest curls.

Let us walk there, only if we must. Step
Lightly. What fell from you I lift

In my hands—through stumbling
Fingers slip your thinnest strands.

2.

Love, the barber, eats down to the roots. Clip, clip.
Yes. I swear the air has teeth some nights

And chews the fields, but not from hunger.
Some bites caress the wound, and heal like death . . . .

My students are cropping their long hair shorter,
Not short, lifting just over their once-covered

Shoulders, their necks still hidden. No ears.
Thought, unspoken, waves through the classroom,

Curls, and in curling, straightens our backs.
My idea, a tight braid, unties, shakes loose.

We are revising our poems. I can be happy to collapse
Into my lines, the furrowing lines in my forehead.

We lift crooked faces. All together—this moment—
We are growing back our lost features.

LAURENCE LIEBERMAN

55

BIOGRAPHICAL NOTES

CAROLYN BALDUCCI   Page 11

Born February 13, 1946, she studied art and photography at Manhattanville College, graduating in 1967. She was a guest editor at *Mademoiselle* magazine, held other editorial positions before moving to the midwest in 1969. Her *IS THERE LIFE AFTER GRADUATION, HENRY BIRNBAUM?* was named an American Library Association Notable Book. She has written another novel, *EARWAX*, and a biography of the Italian Nobel Prize winner in literature in 1926, Grazia Deledda, *A SELF-MADE WOMAN*. In 1975 the author won a grant for the production of her feminist play *ALCUIN*, adapted from the 1798 book by Charles Brockden Brown, the Quaker novelist and reformer. Together with her husband, Gioacchino, she has translated contemporary Italian poets and writers and at present is a writer-in-residence at the Residential College of the University of Michigan, Ann Arbor.

ROBERT BLY   Page 1

Poet, translator, editor and publisher, he was born in 1926. His poems have appeared in many magazines including *Poetry, Chelsea, Ohio Review, Poet* and *Critic, Stone Drum, Field* and *Vanderbilt Poetry Review.* He is the founder and editor of *The Fifties* magazines, which later became the *Sixties,* and *Seventies* magazines, and the *Fifties Press,* (later *The Sixties Press* and *The Seventies Press*) of Madison, Wisconsin. He has translated and published the work of Hans Havass, Georg Trakl, Cesar Vallejo, Thomas Transtromer, Rainer Maria Rilke, Juan Ramon Jimenez and Pablo Neruda. In 1966 with D. Ray, he edited *A Poetry Reading Against the Vietnam War,* and his anti-war poetry readings and talks were widely attended throughout the U.S.A., becoming a signifigant factor in molding public opinion. His most recent work is *Point Reyes Poems,* 1974, and *The Morning Glory,* 1975. He lives near Madison, Minnesota, when he isn't giving readings at colleges and poetry centers in cities here and abroad.

GILLIAN BRADSHAW Page 26

Born May 14, 1956 in Falls Church, Virginia, the poet visited England early in her life, lived two years in Chile, and has majored in English and classics at the University of Michigan, earning a B.A. in 1977. Her *Sonnet XIII* won a Bain-Swigget award in 1975, and in 1976–77 her novel won a major fiction prize in the Hopwood Awards program. Especially interested in Greek poetry, she expects to take a year off before doing graduate work.

E. G. BURROWS Page 41

Although he has lived in Michigan off and on since 1939, this poet was born July 23, 1917, in Dallas, Texas, earning a B.A. at Yale, and an M.A. at the University of Michigan where he won a major Hopwood award in poetry in 1940. His books of poetry include *The Arctic Tern,* Grove Press, 1957; *Man Fishing,* Sumac Press, 1970; *The Crossings,* The New Moon/Humble Hills Press, 1976; *Kiva,* Ithaca House, 1976. His recent poems have appeared in *American Poetry Review, Poetry Now, Poetry Northwest, Epoch, Ascent, Skywriting, Mother Jones, Green River Review* and others. His verse plays have been produced by CBC, Earplay and Radio Nederland. Most of his professional Life has been spent in public broadcasting. He is presently executive producer of WUOM/WVGR, The University of Michigan.

ANDREW G. CARRIGAN Page 53

Born in Battle Creek, Michigan, March 7, 1935, his family moved to a farm near Assyria in the south central part of the state in 1945. After graduating from high school he attended Western Michigan and Olivet colleges, served two years in the U.S. Navy, and returned to earn a B.A. and an M.A. from the University of Michigan. Since 1961 the poet has taught in the Ann Arbor Public School system and for the past four years taught the writing of poetry at the University's Residential College. His publications include *Book 3,* Sumac Press, 1972; and *Babyburgers,* Street Fiction Press, 1975, where he is associate editor. He has read his work several times under the auspices of the

UM Poetry Reading series and on a number of other poetry programs. He lives in Saline with his wife, Susan, and son Jason.

BETH COPELAND   Page 19

A daughter of missionaries, born January 14, 1951, in Fukuoka, Japan, the poet spent much of her childhood in that country, in India and, returning to the United States, in North Carolina. A graduate of the M.F.A. program at Bowling Green State University, Ohio, she currently teaches at Owens Technical College, Toledo, Ohio. Her poems have appeared in *Aphra, Carolina Quarterly, Wisconsin Review,* and other literary magazines and anthologies. She has given a number of readings of her poems at various centers and colleges.

CAROLYN HOLMES GREGORY   Page 38

Born in Rochester, N.Y. on January 27, 1950 "two days after Virginia Woolf's birthday" she was educated in New York and at the University of Michigan where she is a graduate student in clinical social work and psychology. Her poems have been published in *Ann Arbor Review, Art Fare, Astraea, Generation, Contemporary Literature Press, Green House, HERself, Indian, Off Our Backs* and the *Southwest Review.* She has worked as a newspaper editor, for Matrix Theater, and the local food coop work magazine. She has travelled in the South, the midwest, New England and Canada and is presently working on an anthology of writers entitled *Reliquary.*

DONALD HALL   Page 17

Author of more than 30 books, including seven volumes of poetry, several anthologies, an encyclopedia of contemporary poetry, and a play about Robert Frost's work (An Evening's Frost) produced off-Broadway, he was born September 20, 1928, in New Haven, Conn. Educated at Phillips Exeter Academy and Harvard, he earned a B.A. in 1951. In 1952 he won the Newdigate Prize at Oxford, England, where he received a B.Litt. in 1953. He was appointed a Junior Fellow at Harvard from 1954–1957. Poetry editor of *The Paris Review* for nine years, he joined the Department of English at the University of Michigan in 1957. He moved to his Danbury, N.H. farm in 1975. A winner of numerous prizes, fellowships and awards for his work, he has one son and one daughter.

SAM HAMOD   Page 32

This author and teacher was born February 16, 1936, in Gary, Indiana. He earned a B.S. in 1957 at Northwestern, his M.A. from the same university in 1960, and his Ph.D., in 1973 from the University of Iowa. A writer and consultant for television, he is the author of six books of poetry. In addition he has studied at the University of Chicago Law School and taught in the Department of English, University of Michigan, Flint. His work has appeared in a number of anthologies, he is presently teaching in the English department of Rider College, Lawrenceville, New Jersey, and is completing work on a new book of poems.

WARREN JAY HECHT   Page 49

Born in Brooklyn, N.Y. December 31, 1946, this writer received his B.A. from City College of New York, 1969, and has done advanced work at the University of Michigan. He was awarded the CCNY Theodore Goodman Fund grant for fiction, 1969, and appointments as a writer-in-residence, teaching fellow and lecturer at the Residential College, at the University in Ann Arbor from 1970 through the present. His poems and stories have been anthologized in a number of magazines including *Prestare, Anon, Hard Cider Press, The Lake Superior Review,* and the *Michigan Daily Magazine.* In 1974 six of his stories were published in *New Directions Anthology # 29,* New York. He is a director and general editor at Street Fiction Press, Ann Arbor.

BERT HORNBACK   Page 36

Born in Bowling Green, Kentucky, December 22, 1935, the poet and teacher came to the University of Michigan in 1964, after earning three degrees from the University of Notre Dame, and spending a year at

Trinity College, Dublin. He cites as influences on his life "my father who taught me basketball, how to enjoy it intellectually and aesthetically as well as physically; my mother, who taught me to tell stories and design houses and my grandfather, who built a perpetual motion, and let me help him." He organized and ran the U-M Poetry Series from 1968 until 1976 and in 1970 along with Donald Hall and several other people in Ann Arbor, created Poetry Ann Arbor, which for a period of five years sent poets to read in the local schools. He reads *David Copperfield* at least once a year and teaches nineteenth and twentieth century English literature. His poems have been published in nearly a dozen little magazines during the past few years.

LEMUEL JOHNSON   Page 25

Born December 15, 1941, in Northern Nigeria of Sierra Leone parents, the author and teacher has had short stories published in *The Literary Review*, the *Journal of New African Literature* and the anthology *African Writing Today*. In 1971 his study *The Devil, the Gargoyle and the Buffoon: the Negro as Metaphor in Western Literature*, was published by Kennikat Press. He has translated a one-act play by Rafael Alberti entitled *Night and War in the Prado Museum*, as well as the five act play *The People's Dreamer* by the Spanish playwright Antonio Buero Vallejo. The two most recent publications of his poems were in *Third World Voices*, Random House, New York, and the Ardis Publishers, Ann Arbor, Michigan, book *Anthology of New American Poetry*. He is on the faculty of the Department of English, University of Michigan. Married, with a son and a daughter, he has just returned from a visit to Sierra Leone.

GAYL JONES   Page 6

The author, poet and teacher was born in Lexington, Kentucky, November 23, 1949. She has a B.A. from Connecticut College, New London and an M.A. from Brown University, 1973, followed by a Doctorate in Arts from the same institution. Her first novel, *Corregidora* and in 1976 her second, *Eva's Man*, attracted considerable favorable acclaim. She is presently teaching creative writing and Afro-American literature at the University of Michigan. A book of her short stories, *White Rat*, is scheduled to be published this year.

MARGARET KAMINSKI							Page 34

This poet was born March 16, 1944 in Detroit, Michigan. She earned a B.F.A. in 1966, and her M.S.L.S. in 1969 from Wayne State University, Detroit. She operates Glass Bell Press, a women's poetry press in Detroit and has co-edited *Moving Out,* a feminist magazine, for the past seven years. Her first book of poetry was published in 1975 and her second, *La Vida de la Mujer* was published by Fallen Angel Press, 1976. She has travelled in Mexico, South America and Turkey. Most recently she has been working at the Detroit Public Library as a librarian and in public relations where she did radio interviews of authors and produced other radio shows.

JANE KENYON							Page 15

The poet was born in Ann Arbor on May 23, 1947, and educated at the University of Michigan, earning a B.A. in 1970 and an M.A. in 1972. As an undergraduate she received a Hopwood award for poetry and her work has been published in *The Nation, American Poetry Review, The Paris Review, Michigan Quarterly Review* and other magazines. Now living in New Hampshire, she is co-editor of *Green House,* a magazine of poetry. *From Room to Room,* included in this collection, is the title poem of her forthcoming book being published, Fall, 1977, by the Alice James Poetry Cooperative, Inc., of Cambridge, Mass.

MAXINE KUMIN							Page 2

Author of four novels and five books of poems, (most recently *House, Bridge, Fountain, Gate,* published by Viking), the poet was born June 6, 1925, in Philadelphia. She was educated at Radcliffe College, earning an B.A. in 1946 and an M.A. in 1948. She has taught at Tufts University, Medford, Mass., Newton College of the Sacred Heart, Newton, Mass., University of Massachusets and at Princeton University. She won a Lowell Mason Palmer award, a National Endowment for the Arts grant, William Marion Reedy award, Eunice Tietjens Memorial prize, and in 1973, a Pulitzer Prize for her book *Up Country: Poems of New England.* She writes that *How It Is,* which first appeared in the New Yorker magazine, was conceived as an elegy for Anne Sexton. Married, with three children, she lives in New Hampshire and has lectured and read her work on a number of college campuses across the nation.

PHILIP LEVINE   Page 8

The poet was born in Detroit, January 10, 1928, educated at Wayne State there, with a B.A. in 1950, an M.A. in 1955, and an M.F.A. at the University of Iowa. The author of several books, his work has appeared in many publications and he has received many important prizes and honors. He has taught at California State University at Fresno and most recently at the University of Cincinnati, Ohio. He married Frances Artley in 1954 and has three sons. He has travelled widely in the United States, in Spain and Italy and his most recent book, *Names of the Lost,* was published last year by Atheneum.

LAURENCE LIEBERMAN   Page 54

Poet, teacher and lecturer, this author was born in Detroit, Michigan, February 16, 1935 and originally spent a year in medical school. He is deeply interested in the interfacing world of nature and philosophy. He earned an B.A. in 1956 and an M.A. in 1958 from the University of Michigan where he was a major Hopwood winner. His work has appeared in the major magazines including *Atlantic, Harper's, The Hudson Review, The Carleton Miscellany, The Yale Review, The Paris Review* and others. A professor of English at the University of Illinois, he was awarded a creative writing fellowship by the Center for Advanced Study there in 1971 and spent a year travelling with his wife and three children in Japan and Hawaii. In October, 1977, the University of Illinois Press published his collected essays on contemporary American poets, *Unassigned Frequencies: American Poetry in Review (1964–77)*

RICHARD E. McMULLEN   Page 44

Born in Ypsilanti, Michigan, in March, 1926, the writer grew up in the Milan area where he still lives. During World War II and the Korean War he served as a hospital corpsman in the U.S. Navy. He earned a B.A. from Alma College and an M.A. from the University of Michigan. His first collection of poems, *Chicken Beacon,* was published in 1975. He has held a variety of jobs; foundry worker, janitor, newspaper reporter, but since 1956 has worked as an English teacher, presently on the faculty of Pioneer high school in Ann Arbor. Married and the father of three children, he has read his work in a number of schools and colleges. His poems have been published in *Anon, Cardinal Poetry Quarterly, The Massachusetts Review, Northwest Review, Periodical Lunch* and the *New York Times.*

JUDITH MINTY   Page 23

Born in Detroit August 5, 1937, this poet and teacher earned a B.S. in speech at Ithaca College, Ithaca, N.Y. and an M.A. in English at Western Michigan University in 1973. Her book *LAKE SONGS AND OTHER FEARS,* was published by University of Pittsburgh Press, 1974, and she is a recipient of the United States Award of the International Poetry Forum. Other awards include a John Atherton Fellowship in Poetry at Bread Loaf Writer's Conference and the Eunice Tietjens Award, *Poetry* magazine. Her poems have appeared in seven anthologies and numerous magazines including *Atlantic, Poetry, Green River Review, Seneca Revue, The New Yorker, New York Quarterly* and *Sycamore.* She is presently teaching as poet-in-residence at Central Michigan University and helped organize the *Third Coast Poetry Newsletter* and the Poetry Resource Center at Thomas Jefferson College. She writes that she "lives on a sailboat in summer and often hermitizes in the North woods." .

DUANE NIATUM   Page 28

Born February 13, 1938, in Seattle, Washington, this poet spent much of his early life on the Olympic Peninsula. A graduate of the University of Washington, he received an M.A. from Johns Hopkins University. An American Indian, a member of the Klallam Nation, whose ancestral lands are on the Washington Coast along the Strait of Juan de Fuca, the major influence on his prose and poetry is his Indian ancestry. His writing has also been nourished by an increasing interest in all

64

the arts as well as by an exposure to oriental cultures. His poetry has been published in many literary magazines including *The Nation, Prairie Schooner* and *Northwest Review.* His third book of poems, *Digging Out the Roots,* is being published this year by Harper & Row.

JOYCE PESEROFF Page 50

Born in New York City on May 11, 1948, the poet studied at Queens College, N.Y., and worked for *Newsweek.* Later she went to California and in 1969 earned her M.F.A. at the University of California, Irvine. In 1973 she was elected to the University of Michigan Society of Fellows; during her tenure in Ann Arbor she taught a contemporary poetry seminar and directed several independent study projects. Recently she was an N.E.A. writer-in-residence at Marietta College, Marietta, Ohio. Now teaching at a community college near Boston, Mass., her first book of poems, *The Hardness Scale,* is being published, fall 1977, by Alice James Books of Cambridge, Mass. She is co-editor of *Green House* magazine and with her husband lives in Dedham, Mass.

WILLIAM STAFFORD Page 5

Born on January 17, 1914, in Hutchinston, Kansas, with a B.A. and M.A. from the University of Kansas and a PhD. from the University of Iowa, the poet is widely known as a literary critic and writer of personal experiences. He has read all over the United States and is the author of more than a dozen books. In 1947 his *Down In My Heart* detailed his life as a conscientious objector during World War II and since 1957 he has served on the Oregon board of the Fellowship of Reconciliation. He has taught at Lewis and Clark College, Portland, Oregon, 1948-1954, 1957-1960 and as a professor of English at San Jose State College, California, 1956-1957. His *Travelling Through the Dark,* 1962, won a National Book Award and in 1970-1971 he was appointed a Consultant in Poetry at the Library of Congress, Washington, D.C. In 1972 he lectured for the U.S. Information Service in Egypt, Iran, Pakistan, Indian, Nepal and Bangladesh. Most recently he has published *That Other Alone: Poems,* 1973; *Leftovers, A Care Package: Two Lectures,* 1973; and with Kim Stafford, *Braided Apart,* 1976.

Born in Richmond, Virginia, November 4, 1937, the poet attended Davidson College in North Carolina, earning a B.A. there and an M.A. from Harvard. From 1961 through 1965 he taught at William and Mary College, since 1965 he has been a professor of English at Washington and Lee University, Lexington, Va. He is the author of five books of verse, the most recent, *Round & Round* published by L.S.U., 1977. He was poetry editor of *Shenandoah* for more than ten years, his poems have been published in more than 20 anthologies, including *The New Yorker Book of Poems, New York Times Book of Verse,* and *Contemporary Poetry in America.* His articles and reviews have been published in *Modern Language Quarterly, Tri-Quarterly,* and *Poetry.* He has read his work from the University of Hawaii to the University of Maine and to New Orleans.

BOBBEE L. VALLEAU   Page 47

Born August 7, 1954, in Dearborn, Michigan, as a child she lived there with her great-grandmother, later moving to New York (Hell's Kitchen) with her mother, an actress. She worked as a child actress, attending Professional Children's School in New York, Hunter College High School and the Upward Bound program of Queen's College, N.Y. At 16 the poet and performer returned to Michigan, later studying pre-school education at the University of Michigan. A daughter of a jazz musician, she plays the dulcimer, recorder and guitar, is interested in folklore and Native American Indian religious philosophy. She is the mother of a baby son, Justin Earl.

ANNE WALDMAN   Page 42

Born April 2, 1945, "close to noon and in Millville, New Jersey" this poet grew up on Macdougal Street in New York city. She earned a B.A. from Bennington College where she edited *Silo* magazine and began *Angel Hair* magazine and books. As assistant director and director she's been involved at the Poetry Project at St. Mark's Church in the Bowery since 1966. In 1974 she founded with Allen Ginsberg, the Jack Kerouac School of Disembodied Poetics at Naropa Institute, Boulder, Colorado. Author of six books of poems, the most recent are *Fast Speaking Woman* and *Journals & Dreams*. Fusing poetry/drama and dance she has read and performed from coast to coast and abroad. Her work has appeared in many magazines including *Paris Review, Poetry, Rolling Stone,* and *Transatlantic Review.*

REED WHITTEMORE   Page 13

Born in New Haven, Conn. on September 11, 1919, the poet, essayist and literary critic is also a distinguished author, editor and teacher. After World War II in which he served in a support group in North Africa, Sicily and Italy, he joined the faculty of Carleton College, Northfield, Minn. He is the author of more than a dozen books of poems and essays and has served as literary editor for the *New Republic.* He was appointed Consultant in Poetry, Library of Congress, in 1964–1965 and Bain-Swigget Lecturer at Princeton University, 1967–1968. A professor of English at the University of Maryland, his most recent book is *The Mother's Breast and the Father's House.*

NANCY WILLARD   Page 31

This poet, critic, teacher, short story author and writer of several children's books was born June 26, 1936, in Ann Arbor, Michigan. Five of her books of poetry have been published and the most recent of her children's books are *Simple Pictures Are Best,* and *Stranger's Bread,* both published in 1976 by Harcourt Brace Jovanovich, New York. *The Highest Hit,* a novel, will come out in the spring of 1978. She earned a B.A. and PhD. at the University of Michigan where she won a major Hopwood award in poetry; her M.A. is from Stanford. She won an O. Henry award for a short story in 1970 and the Lewis Carroll Award in children's literature in 1977. Married to Eric Lindbloom, she has one son and teaches in the Department of English at Vassar.

ABOUT THIS BOOK   The color cover photographs were taken by the editor near the old Leslie barn in Leslie Park, Ann Arbor, Michigan, at 7:45 a.m. on a January morning when the temperature was five above zero. The camera was a Rollei 35, Honeywell, made in Germany. Speed was 125 at f.5/6. The film was Kodacolor II.

All the other black and white photographs in the book were made using available light, the camera was a 35 mm Leicaflex made by Leitz, Wetzlar, Germany; film, Kodak Tri-X.

ABOUT THE EDITOR

Jeanne Rockwell, who is responsible for the selection of the poets, their poems and all the photographs, was born in Brooklyn, N.Y. January 30, 1920. She has a B.A. in English from Bucknell University, Lewisburg, Pa., studied at the University of Texas, Austin, and earned an M.A. from the University of Michigan, Ann Arbor, in 1974. She has worked as a photojournalist in New York, in five states and as a special correspondent for the Booth Newspaper chain in Belfast, Northern Ireland. Her poems, articles and photographs have appeared in a number of magazines including Christian Century, Friends Journal and the Michigan Quarterly Review.

This book is typeset in 10 1/2 point Univers Medium
by photographic offset process and
Printed by Edwards Brothers
Ann Arbor, Michigan.

Price: $5.00   Additional copies may be secured at your bookseller or by writing
NOON ROCK, 1500 Longshore, Ann Arbor, Mi. 48105

70